CW00518772

JOUISSANCE

Jouissance

WILLIAM SCAMMELL

To Joyce, with best wishes
Bill
5 iii 85

HARRY CHAMBERS/PETERLOO POETS

First published in 1985
by Harry Chambers/Peterloo Poets
Treovis Farm Cottage, Upton Cross, Liskeard, Cornwall PL14 5BQ

© 1984 by William Scammell

All rights reserved. No part of this publication may be reproduced,
stored in a retrieval system, or transmitted, in any form or by any
means, electronic, mechanical, photocopying, recording, or
otherwise without the prior permission of the publisher.

ISBN 0 905291 61 1

Printed in Great Britain by
Latimer Trend & Company Ltd, Plymouth

ACKNOWLEDGEMENTS are due to the editors of *Clanjamfrie*, *Critical Quarterly*, *Encounter*, *Grand Piano*, *The Honest Ulsterman*, *The Literary Review*, *London Magazine*, *New Statesman*, *PEN Broadsheet*, *Poety* (Chicago), *Poetry Durham*, *Poetry Matters*, *The Observer*, *Raven*, and *Times Literary Supplement*, in which some of these poems first appeared, and to the editor of *Poetry Now* (BBC Radio 3).

'The Tall Hedge' was published in *Presences of Nature* ed. Neil Hanson (Carlisle Museum & Art Gallery 1982).

'Broderie Anglaise' was published in *Cloud Station* ed. George Szirtes (Starwheel Press 1983).

'Ten Miles for a Kiss' was published in *Between Comets*: For Norman Nicholson at 70, ed. William Scammell (Taxus Press 1984).

SUBSIDISED BY THE
Arts Council
OF GREAT BRITAIN

Contents

III POINT BLANK

I JUXTAPOSITIONS

' . . . for two dangers never cease threatening the world: order and disorder.'

—Valéry, *The Crisis of the Mind*

Driving Home

I know these big arterial roads
pretty well now, how the wind
swings over bridges, kestrels simmer
on their hob, the crows time
near-extinction to a hop, a step;
know the xerox smell as, heating
up, my car prints out the miles.

I stop as dusk comes on, fill up
and eat my tepid rolls. The coffee's
mashed itself to ashes. Zombies
tuck a thin arm deep in pockets
and their brothers stamp my cheque.

Malvern and Cotswold go by
like darkening ancient liners.
North to south's no problem
it's the getting across country
to my birthplace: what connects
this road and that? I wind my way

across the plain. Dark thatches
every mile, until I hit the flyover
and lights seed their old magic
on Southampton Water, swaying oily hips
up at the lamps' cortège.

I speed past into the city suburbs
limbs like armour, all the shires
packed humming in my head.
The gold watch that I brought from
Curaçao is fastened on your speckly
wrist, turning heirloom by the hour.

Jouissance

Having it both ways
I see, as usual. Praise
to the crucifixion, and the Javanese.

I like those brilliant
white angelic Breton
peasants fluttering bonnets armoured *Bon!*

And though no connoisseur
of colour (since my mother
handed down the fatal gene), the harder

you shout blue, or brown
at breast and sky and hand
to bring the bourgeois greybeards tumbling down

and make red blood
a force for good—
the better to get lost in your symbolic wood!

It's not easy
importing delicacy
into a strict *Fuck off!* Nor, conversely,

getting the great
abstractions on their feet
and clocked on at the factory gate.

Here in the sticks
beyond the Lakes
(that other Cumbria no tourist ever makes

where Frizzington and Cleator Moor,
Pica, Broughton, Maryport
hang on the edge of England) someone saw

three youngsters, sex
writ urgent in their backs,
go fish bright dresses from the letter-box

of someone's new boutique.
The magistrates were speech-
less, Paul, as crows nailed to a copper beech

or Cézanne when (*Salut!*)
you pinched his fruit
and, smiling, murmured 'What's the use of it?'

Hail then
to thee, Gaugin
from the Pension Fund. Bite in. Hang on

and we'll puzzle it out.
Mette sends love and hurt.
Have you found the colour yet from *is* to *ought*?

Finsbury Park

In the mouth of a Scots girl 'polymorphous perversity'
takes on the disinterestedness of chamber music.
She sits in the kitchen telling me about Freud.
It's late. The answering machine is connected up,

Cunning Stunts posters brighten a pillar, couscous
lies in wait for breakfast. There are skips all over
Finsbury Park, swingboats fallen to earth. She will put back
the sky of tumbled ceilings. I go to bed with Thomas Mann

on music: 'Her strictness of form must stand as an excuse
for the ravishments of her actuals sounds.' Basta.
There's something I've always liked about big girls,
their granite jeans, the long slope of unfussy minds.

Contracted to friendship, we have declined
to colonise love's empire. Our forte's thought
whose gender is marmoreal sleep, the god of pulses
running up his storm cones in the dark.

Gainsborough's 'Mr & Mrs Robert Andrews'

Well here's England, breeched and vista'd, all replete
with home and harvest on a cast-iron seat.

The dog looks to the man, the man through us.
The woman's ... vassalage? How barbarous

her dress is to that tree, the gathering sky
whose distant threat highlights propinquity.

And does he own the land? Does it own him?
How many corners to a gentleman!

The set-up will be reaped, her bosom keep
its tryst, grown serviceable to those sheep.

Meanwhile, lace cuffs against that harvest day,
brushed silk, the very fields décolleté

extruding a rush of notions from sheer charm:
propped absolutes conferring, down upon the farm ...

The Tall Hedge

Well they cut down the tall hedge
and burnt it at the field's ending.
What with green sap and mizzling rain
it wouldn't catch at first, so petrol
was brought in. A flame sailed
thirty feet tall, heating me up through
window glass, and the brash cracked cleanly
in the roar. A dozen cows, heads giant
dreamy sycamore seeds, swayed down
to bathe in the smoking ash. I knew
that cows were curious, but not that they
were connoisseurs of red-hot pyres.
For one whole week they anchored in that place
shifting and bumping like fat rowing boats
tied to a pier, and scoffed the lot,
ash, charcoal, mud, gouging a giant lick
where tides of grass now topple under rain.

Retired

Cushions go here,
so. Wednesday's boiled
ham. The blue jug's
only ever used for milk.

Things are said twice
or more, hammered out
like tunes for
your better understanding.

Propped on shining planes
of wood, the children's
children detonate
the family smile.

Air plumps above
the gas fire's hiss;
stiff curtains sentry off
each shorter day.

They slip on proverbs
well-made as leather shoes
in which to sit,
survive the news . . .

I don't know comes
sighing crisply out,
all knowledge flaming
in a single breath.

Woman Painting

A fortune in oils . . .
Inchworms, exotic nouns
of pure colour, the world's
garden on a palette.

She won't paint
for money, won't travel
further than light does.
Her only charge

is silence and peace
which some might think large.
Fancy being her
entranced by a chair

in a window.
Light's her lover
attentive, strong
kissing her all over

without even trying . . .
They stretch out
the afternoon, on tiptoe
together in a room

bereft of winners
till I show up
with coffee, and sugar
in a china cup.

Two dogs, a cat
attend the inquest.
The world is respected.
Her hands are black.

Daphne In The Pathless Wood

'Lord of Delphi, Claros and Tenedos
and of the realms of Patara, son of Jupiter,
past present future are revealed to me!
I am Boulez, Messiaen and Berg
my throat is for all time
I am the Rite of Madison Square Garden
Hippocrates shall swear my oath
I shoot real straight
join my encounter group, I beg you!'

Thin bark enclosed her breasts, her limbs;
hair into leaves, and leaves to seasons' shining;
all her toes, they mined for water,
mole-things . . . she became a pump.
It's an old story. Friends,
we have married beneath ourselves.

Two Riddles

1.
Men rigged my chamfered oak
and fed me glass, commanded
the ghostly world stand still.
Now my nose is into weather,
executions, nudes; dumb horror
speaks to my one vocable.
I imitate the painters, stiffen limbs.
Smiles come at me like refugees.

2.
A siege, a siege; and I'm the engine.
What you hurl at silence! I have slaves
of course, young girls and many of them.
Some stay with me all their lives,
a sort of marriage ... We work well
though I'm not one for out-of-hours
parleyings. At night, poor poll,
they cover me; the warmth dies down.
I'm quiet then.

Broderie Anglaise

White cotton tops
will figure largely
in the afterlife

the svelte couturier's
Schubertiad, heaven
through a needle's eye

In The Dark

Our neighbours wouldn't much care to be loved.
It is a violence on the person. What they mean
these cool promoters of benevolence

is 'Thank you for being with us' —
the TV anchorman at closedown, sooth
and matey with a million darkened rooms.

I, on the other hand, want to know
where you were all yesterday? The day before?
Whose hand? Whose mouth? What burning bush?

And no, there is no last wish. This
will cost you an eye, some teeth
and trouble; a blood-feud at the very least.

A Letter from Cumbria

'Allah is great, no doubt, and Juxtaposition his prophet'
—Clough, *Amours de Voyage*

Dear Sarah, of the north I sing
where curlews screams at night, and bring
late payments on another spring
    and plovers
strut the norsemen's fields, instructing
    this year's lovers.

The lambs, jump-jetting on all fours
above the fells and Yorkshire Moors
are running races, telling yours
    truly how he
might relinquish winter drawers,
    join in the hoolie.

(Though, sad to say, the other night
those who achieved a dizzy height
descended to a nasty plight:
    a freak snowstorm
laid waste the county, icing white
    each tiny form.)

Up here the fields are big and bold,
love and hate have not been sold
or compromised for English gold,
    that bloodless pact
with 'decency', by which the old
    rule every act.

When kids and cows must copulate
no Mrs Whitehouse stands in wait
to morally abominate
    the call to arms
or tiresomely divert the state
    with false alarms.

Callaghan, Wilson, Thatcher, Foot,
Sir Clement This, Lord Keeper That,
the whole great bumbling *apparat*
    of Whitehall, tastes
of beer that's small and rather flat
    from northern wastes.

As for The Crown, that murky glass
compact of classy muck and brass
in which a nation smirks *en masse*
    I wonder when
the wit of James, or Charles's purse
    might come again?

No matter. We see England straight
perched high up on a farmer's gate.
The shires spread out, the map is great-
    ly coloured in
with tea-breaks, gossip, animate-
    d mortal sin

of which the fruit is us, ripe for
bottling into metaphor
and tippling neat, no *nature morte*
    but *bon vivants*
alive to nuance, *en rapport*
    with Adam's haunt.

I'm rambling, Sarah ... (Note how apt
though, that locution is to tact-
ful exploration of brute fact,
    my poem's drift;
no social-scientific pact
    's more than makeshift.)

As I grow older, paradigms
proliferate. Our crooked times
are subject to inhuman crimes
    of reason: we
must hijack all that Samuel Grimes
    vacuity

(ethnologists—we are not geese;
economists—new mind police;
our spiritual ambergris
    cannot be weighed
by butcher or behaviourist-
    ic pasquinade)—

claim back the sovereignty of good.
Good's 'subjective'? So is blood.
No-one I've heard of ever stood
    against transfusion
on grounds of logic, likelihood
    or imminution.

Conceptual analysis
belongs as much to amourists
and sonneteers and anarchists
    and little Amy
as to the cocky scientists
    of *Academe*.

All great art, great science, sees
interdependence, wood and trees
confirming real identities;
    that Leda's swan
feathering apart her knees
    is thereupon

released from single vision, twinned,
subscendent, manifestly limned
in paradox' great fresco, kinned
    yet single too,
godhead and nothing, flesh rescind-
    ing all taboo.

The ancient apple tree enrobes
snows down blossom on the roads.
Cup Final Day: the crowd explodes
    its nuclear song;
Achilles dreams of scoring, Job's
    old right comes wrong

and I embrace integument,
a shocking waist, sweet nameless scent,
the only decent argument
    imagined yet
that God may be beneficent.
    My Juliet

T-shirted, young and strong, commands
direction of these loving hands.
Her elbows, shampoo, love-songs, glands,
    lips, hunger, smile
are potent new reconaissands
    of England's style.

With pearls and hats she has no truck,
her accent never comes unstuck,
the IUD's her only luck-
    y charm; the chains
her mother's mother wore are struck
    from all her limbs.

She reads, she drives, she banks, she wives,
doctors, gardens, races, swives,
spends a dozen useful lives;
    in that domed head
she loops and soars and swallow-dives—
    and so to bed.

Paul Simon, Dylan, ELO;
Jane Austen, Jong, and Lao tse To;
McEwan, Golding, Burgess, who-
    lly modern Amis,
not forgetting Larkin, Hughes, and Lo-
    well's nod to Seamus.

There's Altmann, Truffaut, Olmi, Ford;
Porridge, Sorry, Muppets, Lord
('Civilization') Clark, there's bored
    Sue Ellen,
eyes and teeth put to the sword
    of take eleven.

There's squash, there's jogging, all the means
to sample all the different scenes
or stroll about in pre-shrunk jeans
    and cotton pants
trying out the world's cuisines
    or potting plants.

The O in *love*'s good value, it's
the mother of arithmetics,
the vowel that must always fix
    A poet's stare,
whose *Look!* confounds all Jesuits'
    didactic glare.

I must unlearn that foolish cry
of middle-class propriety.
It is a deadly anomie
    picks England clean;
they'd rather stiffen, rather die
    than 'make a scene'.

I must, I shall, I will, I do
hereby commit my atoms to
the curlew's beak, the sacred cow,
    to nothing less
than seven stomachs, and the plough
    of happiness.

The Wide Blessing

Count me among the sleepers. Nine hours flat
I'm busy not attending to the state.
The world contracts, the black spots all dilate
and I sprawl into darkness like a cat

and hitch the inside fur above my shoulder
tear up the bills, steal warm space from my wife
peel off the backing of my party life
sham dead, then put my fancy to the boulder.

Operator? This is me. Please put me through.
The weird and starry spaces in my ear
grow wider. Gone, as usual. *Who's Not Who*

claps shut, deposits love among the bones
whose weighty serifs print me on the air
regardless, tangible as sticks, as stones.

Documentary

'I cut Babs Rooney but I didn't kill him'
                —Jimmy Boyle

Bend to the screen. A thunderous surf of kids
plucks at the midnight stairwell, washes streets
alive with pointy shoes in gothic suits
and quiffs as razor-sharp as Alan Ladd's.

In tenements, in fortress pubs, the boys
extort a living. When a man is cut
You know the score's diagonally put
in bloody neon across face and eyes.

Then gaol, where art directors run amok:
steel baton boot clash on the inner ear
muddying our balance. Tall screws hit back

with proxy toecaps, bulled to nourish rights
whose grainy pin-points fade into the glare
of deep compassion, and the studio lights.

History

'in contradiction to every known principle of the human mind, that singular people seems to have yielded a stronger and more ready assent to the traditions of their remote ancestors than to the evidence of their own senses'
—Gibbon, *Decline and Fall*, Chap. 15

Not Mau Mau, not Makarios, Korea . . .
Those arrant 'fifties wars made subs reach for
their large, empiric points. Not east of tea
and coffee either, out past diarrhoea
where nouns go begging and still we
can't pronounce them. This is British, core
kith and kin refining on their lease.
What goes in crude to fuel policy
is pumped back in a leaden simile.

They are fighting a war whose end is peace.

Not Beowulf, not Kyd . . . It's cells and ops,
it's shit on walls and brains flocked on a floor.
It's Sean and Billy, riding the cyclops.
And sirens by the dozen at the door.

Against Preening

(*For Christopher Pilling*)

That things are things, and words are other things
is postcards from the dead. I trust they sell
themselves more dearly to the hounds of hell.
I hope Magritte & Co., when Old Nick brings

them nicely to the boil, perks up and sings
out notes, not staves. I hope that Ariel
holds next year's Sprites Convention in the tell-tale
ear of Nabokov, that ilk, whose viewless wings

beat in such pretty voids. May Laurence Sterne,
Borges, Prokofiev, Arp, Stevens, Joyce
learn at their leisure what it is to burn

with a hard gemlike flame. All art is choice
and getting choices right. No storied urn
takes precedence over the sacrifice.

Backing Group

Three microphones jab steel tongues at the light.
Drilling like soldiers, swayed and swaying, strong
to wrestle the great pythoness of song
down harshly jewelled spirals of delight:

bewigged and eyelashed, effigies of lust
set screaming over corpses, tall, tight-arsed,
bright-fingered, coaxing stigmata of sex
to bloom in thigh and cordage, black salt breast:

sworn-in, hopped-up, in tune by proxy with
the mind's demented sirens, feeding off
a continental hunger for sheer myth

these endlessly patrol the borders of
hysteria, that legendary park
whose entrance fee is common or garden love.

The Bridge

Where the brimming river takes a breath
the old stone bridge proposes. Working girls
clap homewards from tall benches; mobster gulls
plane in and stall, bob down to threat

the racing currents. There a castle leans
to moss and postcards, history's mullioned tank;
a car squats useless on the river bank;
the town, as usual, turns its back. Some day it means

to listen to that music, where cut stone
absorbs the sounding glint of water, stirs
one patriarchal foot, consents to moan

a triple nothing in each hollow mouth
pure as a spavined tom. Hark to the spurs
of gender, ravelling the virgin's oath!

Courtly Love

Is it a run of breathless haps
enforces this recension?
Gwen John collates them, hands in laps.

See Beatrice, the two Emilies
blanched whiter than their names,
Virginia, Sylvia, Simone Weil . . .

Such anorexic morals, and the miry
heart's unerring claw. They fatten up
for heaven, they portion our desire.

These are puzzles
certainly, fresh martyrdoms
flooding the palate like peeled fruit—

as though our old, green-handled butter knives
laid neat in their stained plush
might fetch a ransom, change our lives.

Blind Byrn

Michael Byrn, a blind Irish fiddler, was a crew member of HMS BOUNTY; Bligh's regime included compulsory dancing for the men, to keep them fit. When the mutiny broke out Byrn was discovered sitting alone in the jolly-boat (whose planking had rotted) listening to the chaotic events about him.

Voices ... Each with its unknown face.
    Heelclap, birdcry, belief
    torn from its scabbard. Grief
stuns the audit. He could trace
wormed oak, triumphant braille
softmouthed beneath his finger-nail.

The people's voice is sounding, blurred.
    Waves thock and slap
    into a sailor's virgin lap
definitions by the yard.
Their state's unhatched, Platonic force
of justice queers the universe.

Art's in the jolly-boat: right fa-
    ces wrong, all facings stripped
    save Christian's raw apocalypt
of pike and gun, who means to stay
within the rim of islands, known to bless
this hemisphere with fruitfulness.

Bligh must steer what course he can,
    men conjure with
    each topos, myth
of duty, golden houris, man
as mercy-giver. Paradise
refracted through four dozen eyes

facets the lonely ear of Byrn
disfranchised, gesturing astern.

Balancing Act

Always some fat tutelary twisting
green about the heart, champing
the leaf it sits on like a caterpillar
passionate to gorge away its future.

I mean the howl of protest that goes up
at not protesting, and the answering fire
of some old Grandma Bones
who cackles in mind's compound, groans

with hindsight like a scholar racked
with sources. Nothing answers to the facts
of passion's clumsy drill.
Siva waves. The snake goes on its belly still.

Soft quarter-tones divide the shambles
and another day squats slow to earth.
You can see it's endless, first to last,
in the dark slow blaze of the dancer's wrist.

Cotswold Valentine

Village England, where the tribe confers,
regroups. Real jam sits on the altars, furs
the wheatgerm. Bless this house. Bless too
the unearned income of new cottagers.

Our Lord on Sundays speaks an authorised
vernacular of retribution, prized
in every parish. Dust spins through the nave;
black Afric's wide-eyed in the porch. Surprised

to be here, like a sloth full-grown,
Loose Chippings hugs its valley, honeyed stone
anonymous and stylish, chiming with
an English sun's pale scumbled monotone.

The graveyard, packed and growing, swells its girth
nuzzling the old church school. Put down at birth
young bloods in singing robes race through the aisles
to sprawl at length on stony earth.

Which is a country party, raddled, strong
to filibuster, close ranks, talk out long
new-fangled bills of rights, the rights of man
scaled up and howling love's old song.

Small Talk

The smooth, the queasy makings of a smile,
the panting close-up of a woman's tears,
the *Look-at-me's* that make you run a mile—
I've really meant to throw it out for years.

The pyramids of strikers, kissing hands,
the sea-surge of the punters in their cages;
the swelling thighs, the milking of the glands—
Yes, I've been wanting rid of it for ages.

The anchormen, wired up to giant quangos,
the low mimesis, symbiotic pomp
when Minister and Trib play pango-pangos
sticking their sticky tongues out in a swamp

of rotting platitudes and purple fruitage
and Disney crocs, too tired to leave the bank,
and thrice-run vistas of amazing footage—
and no-one's ever made to walk the plank.

The girls, the boys, their limbs plucked by guitars
whirl round and round a sneer, inside a tent
of strutting hips, where bongos and sitars
pound yin and yang into a rude cement.

Heard just a room away, or from the street
you'd think the Martians had beamed down on Gdansk
and lasered every cruiser in the fleet
and beat out Rule Galactica on their tansk.

No thansk . . . But wait, next week they're starting Ray's
great trilogy, there's Ibsen's *Master Builder*,
something on Bronzino . . . One of these days
I'll do it, honest. When I'm wiser, older

and closer to last things, when proximate heavens
attract me not, nor beauty makes me shout,
when Reardon's lost the knack of one-four-sevens
I'll switch off, pull the plug, and chuck it out!

The World's Business

What gets the world's business done
is all right with me. The laird
conducts the salmon through his acres,
pert young choirboys sing their maker's
solemn mass, brickies are on guard
with rule and plumb. Beneath the sun

more's new than not, and likely love's
to do over, pierce both sides, or
miss again. There is no special class
of wickedness, no righteousness
incorrigible, nor leader-writer
with justice inked into his gloves.

Let bankers trade for money still
and mothers spend their pain on birth
and gurus, piercing-eyed, grow blind
for payment of another kind,
slapping their sandals down on earth,
fumbling at reason's farthest till.

Metamorphosis

'Young man, you're idle, cheeky, and a cheat!'
my old maths master said, cadaverous
in brown. Thin as a rod, cheeks sunk, he beat
by a curled lip the looks of Lazarus.
His waistcoats, virtue-tight, bound him to treat
schoolboys as motherless and fatherless.
More bile, per square inch, than a BR shunter,
Re-Armer, Paisleyite, or National Fronter.

My crime, my very face, led to detention.
He prowled the aisles. I caught his livid eye
intent on someone's imminent prevention
or, failing that, a rasping homily.
Next thing I knew, a fist (he'd swiftly clenched one)
had knocked me to the floor where, by and by
my wits sat up and blinked. The world went round
oblivious. What's one more schoolboy on the ground?

'You cheat! You cheat!' His voice comes sobbing back
like some crusader garrotting the heathens
or Torquemada, calling for the rack
because I couldn't do my logarithms
and copied out my neighbour's . . . Paddywhack
a connoisseur of all the youthful middens
was up to double-entry schoolboy banking
and didn't much approve of lateral wanking.

I can joke now—two dozen years have passed,
enough to wind a dressing for that day,
translate poor Paddy off to limbo, guest
of Holofernes, Thwackum, Gradgrind . . . Say
great goddess of instruction! what d'you feast
on now the pedagogue has had his day,
each lamb's dipped in the franchise, and delights
in the lush pasturage of human rights?

*   *   *   *   *

41

London, '61. The birds were singing.
The property boom sent concrete blocks to soar
above the populace, whose ears were ringing
as Stones and Beatles thrashed the summer air
to practise bright new freedoms, known as swinging,
and luck was clothed, and flesh was chiefly bare
as tots and teens said goodbye to austerity
and England shook a leg at all posterity.

I'd come to join the city, after years
of skimming round the world. *New Statesman* small ads
yielded a flat (and morals without tears)
on Haverstock Hill, found with a couple of tall lads,
odd bods in other rooms, a cat, and shares
in a Tudor bath. Drollest of all these droll pads
was a pair of tiny rooms up in the roof: an
intro, as things fell out, to matters *Kama Sutran*.

Just up the hill a bit, had I but known it,
poor Sylvia Plath, behind a dark blue plaque
was busy writing, wondering if she'd blown it,
cursing Mother Cold and Father Luck,
boiling the fat off thirty years of bone, lit
only by flames of incandescent black
whose pall would drift onto each mother's tongue
smudging the taste of home for years to come.

Starved of my proper diet, I broke fast
and hungered round the city, swallowing down
a hundred films, plays, concerts: periphrast
by night, by day a cipher in the town.
In weeks I'd shed my background; see, at last
a haughty traveller on the underground!
storming the citadel, by very force
master of every modish intercourse.

Summoning all my fragments of stray knowledge
I put my fizzing brain to work, my bike
to classes at City Lit and Morley College,
thrashed logic to empiric lookalike.
We talked into the night, we lived on porridge
adrenalin and hope, like any tyke.
I was a compound stomach, in perpetual
peristalsis, bizarrely intellectual

and ravenously earthy. How combine
in Venn or Boole, or any other theory
transcendent yearnings, Kant and Columbine,
Paul Klee, *Je est un autre,* and 'Hello deary'?
I twined the aesthete round the philistine
by turns devout, hang-dog, Byronic, leery
until, like Hamlet, I grew rather ill of these
and cast my lot with unresolved soliloquies.

What boots it . . .? Not a lot, friend, not a lot.
However, that came later. What came now
was endless strands that wove a thickening plot
ands lovely Alice, at Apollo's plough.
I mean, a smashing girl set up Shallot
in those two rooms I told you of; and how
they succoured me, as lily-ponds mergansers,
shall line the rough-cast of my next three stanzas.

She sculpted; and to pay for that she bared all
at Camberwell, where painters painted straight,
not Op, or Pop, Conceptual-Situational
or those huge squares of nothing at the Tate.
I passed her on the stairs—always relational:
see Eliot, amongst others—rather late
one balmy evening, hair up, loosely pent,
ascending to her eyrie in a cloud of scent.

Reader, what could I . . .? So of course I did.
Though put like that it sounds brashly deflationary.
In fact we hovered quite a while, outbid
by shock and bashfulness. Love's dictionary
like Murray's, is so crammed, so thickly-thrid
with oceans of new forms and finds, that rarely
can hands, subject to every known volition
turn up the right, the hoped-for definition.

We talked, we looked (this in her room): we kissed.
This shook the.house. We took our chance in bed.
This covered Greater London in a mist.
'Coffee?' 'No thanks.' We drank ourselves instead.
Ray Charles sang *Georgia*, summer showers hissed
against the skylight; nothing much was said,
no index, contents, footnotes, pagination . . .
Just rhythms, hurled across imagination.

Much ink's been spilt on sex—a blue-black sperm
wriggling about the fancy, impregnating
mind's sullen womb, occasionally brought to term
with pearls and plays, more often celebrating
hegemony: the empire's not for squirm-
ing catacombs of words, concatenating
the murky stuff of wishes, instincts, oughts
slithering about the damp side of our thoughts.

For love and death, that celebrated pair
who tilt at windmills, feed Gross National Products
not at all. Cold comfort and hot air
are very well for Freuds and Jungs and Groddecks
and may help Shakespeare buy the lion's share
and Bunting try the edge of Eric Bloodaxe •
but life, good Lord! is mostly ways to mate us,
not Venus' arms, expressly launched to fête us!

Besides—this is the apogee, my peroration;
this stanza draws you off a bit with bias
like Marxists, drawn to endless confrontation
or ideologists, overly pious—
the fact is, reader, sexual congregation
stands in no need of churches, books, hymns . . . Try as
we may, the myth, the itch it is that rapes us:
once got to bed, Quink! Quink! the magic still escapes us.

We met; we mated. High on Haverstock Hill
where lorries change down, love is thought worth carriage
and I unleashed my backhand on the world
pure chemistry decreed another marriage.
I read, I wrote, played tennis, held my girl
closer than limestone hugs a Cotwold parish.
Knocked down again, this time I won: the awful
mandatory science made plain and lawful!

II THE LITERARY LIFE

'Not to want to say, not to know what you want to
say, not to be able to say what you think you
want to say, and never to stop saying, or hardly
ever, that is the thing to keep in mind, even
in the heat of composition'

—Beckett, *Molloy*

Jean Rhys

Your dresses never kept you warm.
Your dancing seldom kept you fed.
A worse insolence than the waiters'
bowed to right and left. In bed

where most things start and end, you wept
and drank too much (the traveller's rest)
and sank the last two fingers for
the fragrant islands of the past.

Cheap music costs, cheap feelings lie.
Both are good to have. The man
who's got to take the record off
will put the record on again.

They called your number just too late.
You missed the boat, you fluffed the show.
Put your immortal stockings on . . .
Chin up, and cheerio.

Talking Emily Blues

Don't want coffee, don't want tea
Don't want the nineteenth century

Don't want Father, don't want snow
Don't want *Blackwood's*, don't want *Crow*

Don't want breasts, don't want hair
red tongue, carpet on the stair

Don't want pupils, worsteds, keys
doctors. Don't want nights and days

Don't want postcards, don't want moors
Don't want your excuse for tears

Don't want curates dressed in graves
Don't want space in Jesus Saves

Don't want clouds on my breastbone
Here's my needle. Dog, sit down

The Making of Modern Love

1. MEETING

Her eyelids, they were good addresses. Let
her waist ache in a ring. She has a vein
of wit, a mind to govern that large brain.
Young, widowed, beautiful and passionate!
Peacock in name and nature! Rides to horse,
loves music, dancing, theatre, oil paint, verse,
new clothes . . . she severs London with her looks,
her smile; her soul crowds daily to her lips.
Done! George needs love. It says so in the books
queueing up his right arm. The organ skips
into a march, thundering down the scale
as, laughing, Mary puts up her bright veil.

2. PARTING

No house, no money . . . Trapped in growing debts,
watching this world's return on Juliets . . .
They moonlit. Bailiffs haunted every place.
They tried to live with Father's famous face
and learnt what iron laws of custom tense
between the poles of love and commonsense!
And then, and then . . . the Other Man, who lies
far off, at anchor in those lovely eyes.
All turns to absence, bitter woman-loss:
they sheer off out by millionths, like the tide
dumping the egoist on his own cross
to stiffen in the arms of wounded pride.

3. WRITING

In verse, George won. 'Lethe had passed those lips'
he says; death grounds the thunderbolt of sex.
In flagrant life, poor Mary hurried home
contritely, desperate to see their son
whom George clutched to himself, forbidding sight
or sound of her, the fallen Raphaelite.
Broke, broken, sopped in fear, she lingered on
the obverse of *The Death of Chatterton*—
who'd had the decency to break his heart
quick, once and for all, in the name of art.
Balanced in the scales of love and fame
she left the world at last. George wrote to friends
that 'one had quitted it who bore my name.'
The supple fingers moved to make amends.

Phoenix & Co.

I'm reading Lawrence, warming both hands at
his Penguin orange beard. *Take that!*

he cries, and some poor lad in whom the flame
burns low is snuffed out with his winkle curled

and smoking . . . Or the girl who, smelling phlox
with low aplomb, stayed firmly in her art-school socks

is drowned, or burnt, or butchered . . . Life is holy
quick, and dark. Some heavy breathing with a fox

will deconstruct Spinoza nicely. Laymen
may consider pansies, pistils, stamen,

all that strong-arm nature stuff, half-nelsoning
an Isadora posture on the Rite of Spring.

A straight, fine jet of life you understand
not *sickly little shrimps* is on demand

between these covers. Oh, it does reproach you so,
this Pelman-Prussian braggadocio

by Nietzsche out of Frazer.—Teachers covet-
ing sabbaticals and biceps, love it!

Think, while Joyce was courting syntax, echoing
Narcissus' well of notions, and the Possum

rigged a mate up out of Webster's ribs
our man had sole rights on Apocalypse—

a flaming Kleenex, as it were, just right
to wipe the wretched from his earthly sight

forever ... Heavy stuff, this hammering
Life Force, inciting *Götterdämmerung*

in Eastwood and parts west, a sort of grievous
psychic harm, beloved of Fürtwangler and Leavis.

The sap that through the green fuse fires the chaps
cries *No surrender*! to each mother's paps,

floats small flotillas of new gothic myths
to blast the *jeune filles* in their wedded bliss ...

* * *

Hau-Kay! Dark blood and light deductions. Tell the wife
she's nowt but wind and watter, and I've gone for life ...

Brief Lives

i

'He married again in 1630' —Helen Gardner, footnote to Henry King's *Exequy*

Long live the bishop's pious verse
that thuds its grief upon the hearse.
And longer live the human name
restored to context by a Dame!

ii

'On Peckham Rye (by Dulwich Hill) it was . . . he had his first vision' —Gilchrist,
Life of Blake

Six angels in a chestnut tree
stood radiant, sabbatical
fruit of the highest husbandry
on Peckham Rye, by Dulwich Hill.

Holy holy holy. Damn all
varnish on a sunbeam. Will
the Lord exhibit Israel
on Peckham Rye, by Dulwich Hill?

Who names the apple mouths the worm;
his needles cast a sepia frill
and light spills once, and once again
on Peckham Rye, by Dulwich Hill.

iii

HOME AT GRASMERE

Here comes William
abolishing distinction
boring into the fell.

He is jumping
at his mind, feeding
like a trout.

Where is the
Archimedian point
but loss of self?

One draws
to his side
as to a river bank

where clear and deep
resort, the eye numbs
or reiterates

iv

Who sets all the hearts abuzz?
Byron is as Byron does.
Sex for women, wit for men
gossip for the inbetween.

v

He read all night, his cottage light
a star above a sea
that washed up every morning
the remains of STC.

vi

There is a tall man far away
    who sings the saddest songs
and sells a thousand books a day
    to love's pale myrmidons.

Ay me, ay me! the energy
   roused up in him by death!
The tears and sighs from mouth and eyes
   the honey on his breath

might raise guffaws from Carlyle
   that Scottish bag of wind
but rivalled Dickens' mad smile
   and whipped the coppers in.

A thousand miseries in his sight
   moved him to utter curses
transmogrified to pure delight
   in crystalline new verses.

Love is death! and sex is death!
   and death is all around!
and death's a sound investment—
   or so our Alfred found.

vii

A gent's sad urge, a lady's muff
tiptoed to the pen of our friend Clough.
O muffled doubt! O sinful shroud!
O Rome! O home! O me! O Claude!

How pleasant to see that Victorian guff
swept away in the sea-surge of Arthur Hugh Clough.
How rightful, delightful, how ripping and topping
when Clough goosed a virgin and said *I'm not stopping*!

Tennyson? Browning? Hopkins? Stuff!
My man's Mr A. H. Clough.
Quatrains? Blank verse? Storm-and-ravage?
Hexapody, in Anglo-savage!

Who brought a whiff from a brand-new whuff?
Who called the age's Blind Man's Bluff? ˙
Who ran rings round the public-school tough?
My school song is: Arthur Hugh Clough.

Arthur, I've just one teeny complaint.˙
It made me hot, it made me faint
when you, of all people, were snide, rude, laid-
back and cutting about people in 'trade'.
Arthur, it's snobbish, a vulgar tantrum.
Where d'you think *your* money came from?

viii

Old Possum wore a pin-stripe suit
    and other sorts of wheezes
like quoting Sherlock Holmes, and then
    evaluating cheeses.

A John the Baptist *de nos jours*
    fox-trotting with the language
his contumeley—worn *de rigueur*—
    wrapped round him like a bandage.

The Buddha grabbed his old young mind
    women grabbed for more.
He stored them in the lamplight
    with old poets and their lore

and watched as all the lamps went out
    and all those poets wept
and wrote a learned paper on
    creative etiquette.

RIP THE BEATLES

Pla ce bo
  Who is there, who?
Oo bla dee
  You love me

Wah wah, the sea, the sky
Rousseau, Jarry, plectrum pie
One two gotta girl
she's the oyster and the pearl
three four silver hammer
nail the knell of Hamlet's stammer

Gus ti bus
  Oh what fuss
Blame bam bam
  What I am

Yeah yeah, the moon, the sun
Jimmy Cagney's got his gun
Make it love, make it war
power to the blue guitar
Home is heaven, chord of C
see ya later. Oobladee

The Age of Alcohol

(For Frank Tuohy)

Washed up in a joint
Minton, Colquhoun and MacBryde
crossed the Red Sea in a pint
and seldom reached the side.

Dylan, Brendan, Myles and Pat
bless this sober habitat

Louis ruled the bar
Tambi covered the loss
Beauty and the Beast walked in
on the arm of MacLaren-Ross

(for girls, where talent gathers
to lay its silver waste
pick up elective fathers
with bold unerring taste).

MacCaig, MacDiarmid and Mother Machree
bless this house and keep it dry

'Where are the new Sassowenbergs?'
Potts was there in a Treece
Spender put the fires out
Orwell kept the peace

Cyril promised promise
Wystan made a boob
Sweeney tasted solace
Henry watched the tube.

East south north west
life's a blackout, beer's not best

The fleet, the fleet was sinking
but Fuller and Ross held on.
Plain living and high thinking
passed out in the back saloon.

I write it down in a weal of woe:
Wheatsheaf and Granby and French
The Swiss, The George, The Horseshoe
The Mandrake, the Whore's Lament.

The muse was not amused—
she said through icy lips
that neither a night on the booze
nor a limp apocalypse

was her idea of living;
she'd rather read *The Waves*
or book a person-to-person
three minutes with Robert Graves.

Make it new, make it behovelier
but lead us not into Fitzrovia

And while the roaring boys
warred nightly, Alun and Keith
saw a generation's joys
die a hasty, measured death.

For the snug's commenced a jungle
the catkins weep in browns
like the heavy-duty dirndl
round Mollie Panter-Downs.

Where the whisky chasers go
send not, send not to know.

Piper picked the ruins
Priestley sang amen
Paul Nash was issuing coupons
Charles Madge was counting men

Balloons went up, the sky came down
someone spiced the lees
as Myra struck Beethoven
right between the keys.

Dylan, Brendan, Myles and Pat
goodbye (again) to all of that

ENVOI

We soldier on without you
our tipple's violence, bigger bangs
though some few still salute you
with awkward hands

Famous Poets

We formed a group, expressly to espouse
the living voice, and met in Wordsworth House

of noble frontage, earnest to imbibe
such idiolects as magnify the tribe.

So, kitted out in verity and ruth
and compasses and brandy, bound for Cockermouth

a clerisy of poets brought to bed
the best that they had thought and felt and said.

The dandies joked, the stoics stood affronted.
The vox pops, shy of brow, all *fuck*-ed and *cunt*-ed.

Mute as a landscape, still as winter reed
packed audiences waited for a seed

and shared good dumbness, wondering at the row
of parallels fronting a poet's brow.

Between, before and after, meeting trains
or dining on the great man's starry brains

we peer into the life, whose shadowed fame
lurks somewhere in the binary of a name.

My wife, the litmus test, pronounces: he
(or she) is of the species still; or wants to be.

In The Province of X

The droshky's late, the birches shine.
Mitya's *Devil take you!* line
resounds through chapter 29.

He'll never get to Masha now
whose profile nods at the exergue
of newly minted Petersburg.
All the Russias stiffly bow

pawing a vodka from the air

as life—'What is it? What is love?'
'Your move, I think, Count Sovalov'—
kippers itself upon the stove.

'You jest, Prince!' 'Count, I never joke!'
The governess learns to revoke
while someone in an Oxfam cloak

adjusts his eyepatch, quoting Pushkin,
fingering his home-made pushpin . . .

'Masha, will you marry Sasha?'
Giggling, Katya almost bursts.
Upon my word, there lies the dacha!
Lightly, lightly fly the versts!

Porfiry shuffles into view
punctually, as good as new.
'Young master, is it really you?'

and frost begins to slipper all
those ghostly figures at the ball—
La vie en Russe
acute, obtuse
tossing its ringlets at the ball.

'*Enchanté,* Princess. I trust
my young men laid siege to your bust.
One or two, whose patronyms
adorn them yet, mislaid odd limbs.
The motherland . . . We must not stint.'
'But how their decorations glint!'

Out upon the boundless plain
the larks are scrambling once again.

'Comte has shown . . . Now Katya, listen . . .
Who has ever touched a soul . . .?
How your eyes begin to glisten!
Ouf, it's hot! Let's take a stroll . . .'

Icily, the Neva chatters.
Peter's horse rears at the gloom.
Porfiry sweeps up these matters
with a large, historic broom.

III POINT BLANK

'You must aim the imagination also at
yourself, point-blank'
  —Saul Bellow, *Herzog*

The Right Distance

You can see how the sheep
got his star part in the book,
at once literal and symbolic.

He is a remedial learner
set inside a barrel of curls,
teacher's pet, likely to bolt,
certain to cast no casting vote.

Stones and trees are his peer group.
A polite lip, and mother's teeth.
After two more deaths I walk
in the direction of the sheep—

real sheep, believe me, who stare
at the goggly stranger standing there.
We magnetise each other
for some minutes, pass and re-pass . . .
exactly the right distance between us.

Dame Nature

Dame nature gives orders to genius
for milk in bottles, geometric fields
babies prinked all over smiles
and a rule of thumb for happiness.

Let there be donkeys, bluebells, crates
of vegetables that clean one's teeth,
starry pelts stretched over brutes,
forgetfulness, and hymns to death.

Make me a stuff that holds in rain
and lets out sun little by little.
Invent the woodstove and the kettle.
Summon the swallows home again.

Name presidents and kings their price
for living loud and talking nice.
Dress the beech in his best bark.
Toughen the skins of those who work.

Let stones and pools and tide-wrack be
miniatures of the galaxy.
What we make of them, call years;
what we might have, common tears.

Ten Miles for a Kiss

'One of the grand
spectacles of the universe'
is Reverend Francis Kilvert
taking his bearings among

'these mountain beauties':
Prissy Prosser, Hetty Gore,
Polly Greenway, Gipsy Lizzie,
Emmeline, Lucretia, Jenny Dew

adjectives bubbling down
the reaches of his eye . . .
Hard by Capel y Ffin
where monkish men

are sweating in
their habits, digging
deep to build, a girl
sings at her washbowl

'up to the elbows
of her round·
white lusty arms
in soapsuds.'

Cwm and dingle, moon
frost, dew, mesmeric
glut of light
upon Plynlimmon

and on fallers
bedded in lush grass
receive their blessing
from the midmost centre

of a curate's heart
whose calling card's a cowslip
tendered to the warm
snout of a latch.

The 'pure fair sweet
grave face' of Annie Dyke
is not at home today:
'ten miles for a kiss'

he'll just have
to imagine . . . and
he will. The air is fat
as a baby's wrist,

unlike Cornwall, where
'the smell of fish is sometimes
so terrific as to stop
the church clock dead.'

Noses notwithstanding, nor
the 'concubinage' of Myra Rees
nor clergyman's daughters
out castrating lambs

('I forgave them')
nor May Eve witches
old and young ('the young
. . . are welcome')

nor a starving cat
that perches in the hovel
of old Pritchard's
guttering life

nor drunken fair days
nor the parish pauper
after a lifetime's labour
slashing his gizzard

to haul out the keck . . .
there's archery and croquet,
boating, picnics, racy
novels by Ouida

('how that woman hates
her sex'), beacon-haunted
Hay-on-Wye hugging
its golden pelt

where mayflies
stitch their cope
in the setting sun
and, after rain, the river

flashes off
like a frightened snake.

Whiteout

(for Chris & Sylvia Pilling)

After the meal and the jazz and the conversation
which requited a Cumbrian Saturday winter evening
the front door opened on an unbid tempest
of intemperate wind and snow, chthonic chaos
storming about the lamps, a whole demented sky
in self-analysis, singing as it bounced on by
past Skiddaw, Greta Hall and Loughrigg Ring
as though it meant to warn and waken everything
with its sublime erratum, whatever that might be
or, failing that, with literal sublimity.
Once in the car, it threw itself upon the lights
upon the windscreen, upon warm-brandied hearts
much like some alien howling to be let in.
We crept into the storm, we inched along
until we met its heartbeat, this sort-of bliss—
the whole universe converging smack on us
one piece at a time, the time continuously now
the now a life and likeness of incorrigible snow
that waited half a friendship pointedly to sharpen
the meal and the jazz and the conversation.

Point Blank

Not a grey hair
in his head. Never
a day's illness.

Charms to conjure with,
but when the X-ray spoke
he wasted quick.

Widowed now, your best friend
followed after; pain
was like a tune

her eyes sunk back
in search of. So
when the breast

you'd lost cried
to its root
and doctors missed

the knack of talking
straight, you wrote
I am a coward

please forgive me
on a buff envelope
and took your cure

of alcohol and pills.
Alas, the day
came queerly back

and you awoke
in one of those dread
barracks of a hospital

you'd hated all your life
where cheerful men
mix cocktails

for the sick.
We have no rites
except to float

the mind off on a raft.
It comes to rest
not in some otherworld

but this one,
run aground here
where no dove returns.

*   *   *

The ground is staked
with headstones, grass
and petals fretting

in the cuff of stone.
Mind cannot climb
down, any more

than it can know
a flower's death.
Which way does

she face? a small
girl said. *I'll plant some
in her bellybutton.*

A dead face
faces nowhere. It rides
a withered stalk, a thing

contingent merely;
can go anywhere.
Hence Leibniz' terror

mocked at by Voltaire.
Who will explain
the sappy haemorrhage

of love? The reek's
soon gone, but not
what it attached to,

not the *is* time
loves to overset.
Reason can't renegue

yet dizzies
stooping to
the lapidary block

where abstract, comfy
lichens breed
their coral of remorse.

Into Our Heads

(I.m. Pete Laver)

My neighbour died in his armchair
aged fifty-six. It was Boxing Day.
Nothing to say why then, why there
two shakes after wetting the tea.

Pete dropped baldly on Scafell
walking one minute, dead the next
at an age neither biblical
nor glossed by any text.

It dins in our ears, crumples the eye.
It steals a day from its normal perch.
It grabs the legs from under pay
thinning a voice to fill a church

where all's one voice, or would be, were
there comfort in a shared defeat,
anything new to be read in terror,
wisdom in getting to your feet.

Air crisps to autumn, buttering fells
whose far-off beauty means to fly
into our heads with taller tales
than any we have told today.

The Billiard Player's Soliloquy

My hand provokes a civil war—
Turneresque sunsets, the doomy kiss
sweet Chekhov blows the old régime—
then fiddles music on its bluntened spear.
Grown to be a father I tolerate
locked bathrooms and a blizzard of denials.
The Two Cultures interested me once,
mine and other people's. I chose
glittering Pascal. Together we overset
buckets of intellectual slop
and rode into the bibliographies.
(Foolishness still upsets me
but the good life is not to be argued for.)

I play all the positions
in the team simultaneously,
close to the wind of every skill.

The balls pulse out a morse
that spells delight, or career
round the angles like boys on bikes.
When I think of Eden I see
a large expanse of green baize cloth
with pockets like old swallows' nests,
a dancing trinity of red and white
and an old gentleman (wearing
slightly soiled white gloves)
keeping the all-important score.

Quatorze Juillet

Good times come in a summer dress
flaring about these sunny limbs
whose nearly naked drama swims
in a breaking wave of undistress.

Cicadas race their spectral lure,
kingpin waiters rule the bar;
it's an eye for an eye, a pound a beer
and Bastille Night on the Cote D'Azur.

Sports cars honk; the girls, the boys
smiling in their walk-on parts
raise consciousness to one of the arts
sparkling along the avenues.

And you, old bachelor husband, hopped up
on a child's love of beauty, facing the blue-
black Med, entranced by the view
as one of the chosen in Noah's ark—

where do you fit? do you fit at all?
Are the fireworks racketing over the sea
blazing an instant, to blaze for me?
Great thunderheads begin to crawl

above the bay; the wind unfurls;
all's weird, electric. Lightning and rain
scatter new magic through the town.
Under the awnings scamper girls

more lovely-damp than dew, thrown sheer
past the waiters' gross imperative
to civilisation's 'What'll you have?'
shawled in the epic stuff of tears.

Ancient and Modern

Back in 1950
when Mums did Palais Glides
and girls still got an earful
from Dad's short back and sides

and creamy capuccino
overlaid the tongue
with sweet and sexy flavours
and pop was Jimmy Young

and sweets came off the ration
and jazz sprang up in dives
and Comets screamed on newsreels
and Woodbines came in fives

and Tories ruled forever
and Empire meant Free Trade
and intellectuals took their stand
in corduroy and suede

and BBC announcers
said Churchill won applors
and Rank rebuffed Jane Russell
with young Diana Dors

and George gave way to Lizbet
and LPs offered gems
as the Festival of Britain
played sweetly by the Thames

and Compton creamed the bowlers
and Longhurst opened up
and Sunset fell at Beecher's
and Matthews won the Cup

and Lady Docker's Daimler
glistened in the mews
and Beaverbrook lost Suez
and Dylan found his muse

and Humph blew infant solos
and Eden made it clear
that only a rich man ever earned
a thousand pounds a year

they brought *you* into being
yes, eyes and nose and chin
all set to smile and play, as if
the past had never been

and parents were for leaving
and history was bunk
and every kind of loving
was money in the bank!

Golden Dawn

A backhand slice is but a paltry shot,
no backbone in it, *sauve qui peut,* unless
hit to the corner baseline, asymptote
plus malice, Pinterishly-primed duress
allowing one to charge in, tête-à-tête,
and do a hotshot number at the net.

When I was young and skinny, I'd not weight
enough to terrorise the baldest ball.
Now that I'm thick, and wise, and roseate
and compact of the waist chimerical
the drop-shot wounds me, and the high lob pains.
Either the body's lacking, or the brains,

it's never damn well right. And that's a shame.
O sages in your manuals, Kenny, Fred
come be the singing-masters of my game,
that ace-tormented serve, weak overhead!
Iron out my faults. Let these joints thrive
and put some bottle in my cross-court drive.   ·

Once in the rankings I shall never smoke
or swear, raise hell at discos, quarrel, swank.
If I can have a swimming pool, and clock
odd starlets on the brink, own my own bank,
I'll bow out gracefully, by fame paroled,
and sit up in the stands as good as gold.

NOTES

'Jouissance': 'you pinched his fruit': see Gaugin's 'Still Life with Profile of Charles Laval'. Last line: David Hume first questioned the propriety of moving from factual or descriptive judgements to value-judgements in *A Treatise of Human Nature,* Book III, Section I, 'Moral Distinctions not Derived from Reason'; and philosophers have continued to argue the point. My own views mays be gathered from stanzas 13 and 14 of 'A Letter from Cumbria.'

'Daphne in the Pathless Wood'. Apollo, who speaks the opening lines, was 'the god of light ... and so of inspiration ... also the dazzlingly splendid young Lord of music and song ... he was the giver of prophecy as well. He was also the healer of bodies with medicines ... he is dread and strange, as well as beneficent ... ' *Myths of the Greeks and Romans*, Michael Grant (Mentor) pp. 121–2.

'Two Riddles'. (i) camera (ii) typewriter.

'A Letter from Cumbria'. IUD: Intra Uterine Device, a contraceptive.

'Documentary'. Suggested by a Scottish Television reconstruction of the life of Jimmy Boyle, who was gaoled for murder.

'History'. *Beowulf*: Old English epic poem. Kyd: Elizabethan dramatist (1558–94) who inaugurated the vogue for revenge tragedies.

'The Making of Modern Love'. Meredith married Mary Ellen Nichols, the widowed daughter of Thomas Love Peacock, in 1849. In 1858 she ran away to Capri with the Pre-Raphaelite painter Henry Wallis. Meredith is thought to be the model for his best-known painting, *The Death of Chatterton*. When Mary returned to England Meredith refused to see her, or to allow her to see their child. She died in 1861. *Modern Love* was published in 1862. For a sympathetic account of Mary's life, see *Lesser Lives* by Diane Johnson.

'Phoenix & Co'. The italicized quotations in the seventh couplet are from Lawrence's story 'The Fox'.

'Brief Lives', ix, 'RIP the Beatles'. The opening is imitated from Skelton's *Phyllyp Sparowe*.

'The Age of Alcohol'. For a survey of the period, see Robert Hewison's *Under Siege: Literary Life in London 1939–45* (Weidenfeld & Nicolson), to which I am indebted for the names of Fitzrovia's favourite pubs.

'The Right Distance'. Written in memory of two friends who died within a few weeks of each other: Sue Bourke, aged 38, and Pete Laver, aged 36.

'Dame Nature'. Suggested by an illustration to the *Romance of the Rose*, 'Dame Nature giving her orders to Genius'.

'Ten Miles for a Kiss'. All quotations are from the Penguin edition of Francis Kilvert's *Diaries*.

'Point Blank'. 'Hence Leibniz' terror ... ': Leibniz argues, in *The Monadology* and elsewhere, that there are no contingent truths, only logical ones; everything that is the case is necessarily the case. Voltaire mocks this doctrine (much as Peacock later travesties Kant and the English Romantics) in Doctor Pangloss's celebrated optimism in *Candide*: 'All's for the best in the best of all possible worlds.'

William Scammell was born at Hythe, in Hampshire, and left school at fifteen. He worked for ten years in various factories and offices, and then as a photographer, before going to university as a mature student. He is currently Newcastle University's Staff Tutor in Literature for Cumbria, where he now lives. He is married to a painter and has two sons. In 1982 he received a Cholmondeley Award from The Society of Authors. His first *Peterloo* collection, *Yes & No* (1979) has sold out, but his second *Peterloo* collection, *A Second Life* (1982)—see back cover for review notices—is still available in both hardback (£4.50) and paperback (£3.00). William Scammell introduces and reads a selection of poems from his three *Peterloo* collections on *Peterloo Poetry Cassette No. 2* (£6.00 including accompanying text booklet).